D1524380

Making Adorable Clay Animals

Cute Clay Animals for Kids

Copyright © 2021

All rights reserved.

DEDICATION

Contents

How to Make a Clay Cat

Creating clay animals is so much fun and makes a perfect hobby or training exercise for budding artists. You can use clay to make any animal or object you can think of or imagine, but this article focuses on a clay cat.

Steps

1

Gather clay, tools, and some big black beads. Get the clay colors that speak to you when you envision the cat. Good choices might be brown, black, pink, red, and yellow clay. You will add interest by creating details with tools such as forks, plastic knives, garlic pressers, whatever your imagination brings forward. The varied textures and colors will make your creature eye-catching.

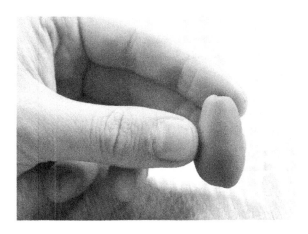

2

Start by rolling out a big piece of brown clay and forming it. This will be the body. Roll the brown clay in a big ball. Then squeeze the top sides a little to create an egg-shaped body.

To add more detail to the belly, flatten a piece of pink clay into an egg shape, a bit smaller than the body. Then stick it on body for the stomach.

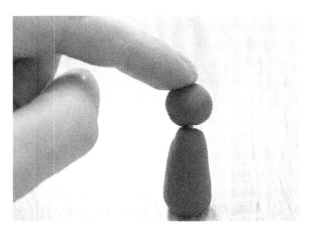

3

Roll a ball of brown clay for the head. Use something to keep it in place, such as a toothpick, when you stick it on top of the body.

4

Make cheeks by flattening two small balls. Put them next to each other on the bottom of the head (not all the way at the bottom). Add a very small ball under the cheeks in the middle.

5

Add the nose on top of the cheeks in the middle.

6

Add eyes using the black beads. You don't really need to make a mouth though because the snout forms the mouth.

7

Make small triangular-shaped ears and poke a small hole in them (not all the way through). Put some pink clay inside the holes and stick the ears on top of the head.

8

Drag a toothpick on the sides of the snout to make whiskers. You can also stick in string to make whiskers.

9

Make front legs. Bend a little at the front to make paws. Add claws by pushing a line down on each paw with a toothpick three times. Stick them on the front of the clay cat.

Do the same method with the legs, but stick them in the back.

Add pads on the arms and legs to add more detail, but you don't have to if you don't want to.

10

Add a tail on the back at the bottom.

11

Finished.

How to Make a Standing Tiger Out of Clay

Clay is fun to work with. You can make almost anything out of it; animals, objects, and more things. This article will talk about how you can make something out of clay in the animal "category", tigers.

Steps

1

Find a flat, clean workspace to create your clay tiger. If you create it on a bumpy surface, the tiger might look bumpy or some parts smaller than the other, for example, the head is bumpy or one leg is bigger than the other. A flat space will help you make your clay tiger comfortably.

2

Start with a big piece of orange clay. Roll it into a ball. Shape it into a rectangular prism. Round the edges to help it look like a tiger's body.

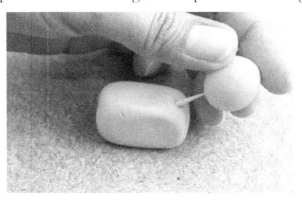

3

Roll a smaller piece of orange clay into a ball. This will be the head. Stick the head at the end of the body with a toothpick.

To stick the head on, break a toothpick in half. Poke one of the halves of the toothpick in the place you're going to put the head. Stick the head onto the toothpick. Don't let any of the toothpick show up at the bottom, and make sure the toothpick doesn't stick out. The toothpick will help the head stay and not fall off.

4

Roll two small yellow balls of clay and add them to the bottom (not all the way at the bottom) of the head. Poke small holes in them.

5

Roll another small ball of yellow clay, and add them under the two muzzles, in the middle. You will see a mouth form.

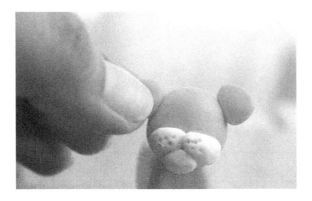

6

Roll two small orange pieces of clay into two balls for the ears. Flatten them, but keep them a little thick. Stick them on top of the head, one on the left, one on the right.

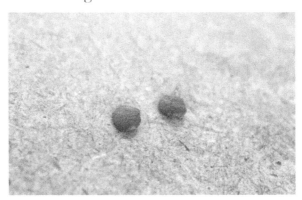

7

Flatten two smaller pieces of black clay, and flatten (this time, not thick at all). Stick them on the front of the ears. These will show the inside of the ear.

8

Make eyes using two small balls of black clay. Stick them on the (not all the way on the top) top.

9

Add a nose using pink or black clay. Shape a ball of clay into a triangle and stick it in the high middle of the snout (where the muzzle and mouth are).

10

Make arms by rolling two cylinders of orange clay. Stick them to the front sides of the body.

11

Bend the end for paws. If you'd like, you can add pads and/or claws.

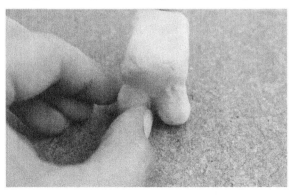

12

Make legs by rolling two cylinders of orange clay. Bend the ends to create paws. Stick the legs to the back sides of the body.

13

Make a tail by rolling a cylinder of orange clay into a thinner cylinder. Roll a black oval of clay and stick it at the end of the orange strip. Stick it where the bottom will be.

14

Make lots of strips of black clay. Stick them everywhere (not all over, or the tiger will be messy!) for stripes.

15

Finished.

How to Make a Clay Bird

You don't have to be an artist to make cute birds out of clay. In fact, you'll probably be surprised when you see how easy it is! Whether you'd like some new decorations for your home or want to try a new arts and crafts project with your kids, molding birds out of clay is the perfect activity. If you'd like a lifelike bird, you can mold three-dimensional shapes to make a small figure. If you prefer a simpler project or are working with your kids, then you can also use a cookie cutter to make easy, flat birds.

Method

1

Shaping a 3-D Bird

1

Scoop out a piece of clay about the size of an egg. Whether you're using clay in blocks or a container, scoop out an egg-sized piece to make the bird's body with. You can use a different amount of clay if you want to, but this amount should give you a bird that fits nicely in your palm, so it's perfect to start with.[1]

You can use any color of clay that you want to. If you use plain white clay, you could always paint it later on to give your bird some extra decoration. Use acrylic paint, which is best for clay.

The size of the clay you start out with isn't super important. If you want to make a bigger or smaller bird, then just use a different amount of clay.

Any type of modeling clay that you'd find in a craft store will work for this. You might want to get a few different colors for the different parts of the bird.

2

Roll the clay into a ball between your palms. Hold the clay in between your palms. Then roll the clay between your palms by making small circles with your hands. Don't press too hard or you'll crush the clay. Stick with light pressure. Keep rolling until the clay forms into a ball.[2] The ball doesn't have to be perfectly round.

3

Mold the clay into a teardrop shape. Now give the bird's body some shape. Pinch one end of the ball to thin it out. Imagine you're trying to make the ball into a teardrop shape. The thinner end is the bird's tail.[3]

If you mess up at any point, just roll the clay back into a ball and start over. Any mistakes are really easy to fix.

4

Bend the tip of the teardrop up to make a little tail. Hold the thin end
of the teardrop between 2 fingers. Bend it up a little so it forms a little
tail for your bird.[4]

You can bend the tail as much or as little as you want. Bending it up a
lot gives your bird a very pronounced tail, like it's in flight.

5

Roll another clay ball about 1/3 the size of the bird's body for its head.
Put the bird's body to the side and scoop out another piece of clay.
Make it about 1/2 to 1/3 the size of the bird's body. Roll it into a
round ball like you did for the bird's body to make a perfect head.[5]

You can always add more clay or take some away if the size of the head
isn't right. It's easy to fix if you don't like the size at first.

6

Press the head firmly onto the thick end of the body. Take the head
and gently press it onto the side of the body opposite from the tail.
Hold it for a second to make sure it sticks. Now your bird has a head![6]
Don't press too hard when you stick the head on or you could crush
the bird's body.

You can leave the head rounded, or mold it a bit so the borders blend with the body. This makes your bird look more lifelike. It depends on the look you're going for.

7

Poke 2 holes in the head for the bird's eye sockets. Get a pen or toothpick and poke holes on either side of the bird's head to make eye sockets. Depending on the size of the bird, the pinpricks could be large enough for the eyes, or you might want to widen them a bit if your bird is bigger. This helps the clay eyes stick better later on.[7]
Do your best to make the eyes even on each side. Otherwise, bird's eyes will look crooked.

8

Add 2 small clay balls for the bird's eyes. Scoop out 2 tiny pieces of clay, about the size of the 2 eye sockets that you made for the bird. Roll each piece between your fingers to make them into little balls for the eyes. Then gently press an eye into each socket. Don't press too hard or you could knock the bird's head out of place! [8]
You can use all different colors for all of these detailed pieces. For the eyes, you might want to use black or a similar dark color.

If you prefer, you could skip this step and just leave the eye sockets empty. The little holes also look like eyes by themselves.

9

Mold a little cone for the bird's beak. Scoop another piece of clay, about twice the size of the eyes. Hold the clay between your fingers and roll it into a little cone, so one side is thinner than the other. Then take your little beak and angle it so the thicker side is facing the bird's head. Gently press it onto the front of the head to give your bird a beak.[9]

If you want to use a different color for the bird's beak, yellow or orange are good choices.

Don't worry if the shape isn't perfect. As long as it's a little thinner at one end, it will make a great beak.

You can make a little slit with a knife if you want the beak to look like it's open.

10

Make 2 flat teardrop shapes for the bird's wings. Use 2 more small pieces of clay. Flatten each one out so they can cover about half of the bird's side section. Then pinch one end of each piece to mold it into a flat teardrop shape for the bird's wings. Press a wing onto each side of the bird. Hold each one for a few seconds to make it stick. Now your bird looks like it's ready to fly![10]

You can also use different colors for the wings, or just the same color as the bird's body.

If you want your sculpture to harden, then leave it out to dry. Different clay types have different drying times, but most clay should harden within 24 hours.

Method

2

Making a Flat Clay Bird

1

Flatten an egg-sized piece of clay onto a table. Take clay of any color and break off a piece. Roll it out on a table, then flatten it out so it's a little bigger than the cookie cutter that you're using.[11]

You might want to work over a placemat or on a cutting board so you don't make a mess.

If you have trouble getting the clay flat enough, you can use a rolling pin to help.

Any type of modeling clay that you'd find in a craft store will work for this.

2

Press a bird-shaped cookie cutter into the clay. Get the cookie cutter and center it over the clay. Then press it down to cut a bird shape into the clay.[12]

Brid-shaped cookie cutters are easy to find online or in craft stores.

If you don't have a cookie cutter, you could use a knife and cut a bird shape into the clay.

3

Peel away the excess clay around the cookie cutter. After cutting the bird into the clay, there should be some extra clay outside the bird. Peel this away so you're just left with a bird-shaped piece of clay.[13] Save the extra pieces of clay. You can do other crafts with them.

4

Draw an eye and a wing onto the bird with a pen or toothpick. Decorating your bird is easy. Just get a pen, toothpick, knife, or stick to start. Then poke a hole on the bird's head for an eye. To give your bird a wing, simply draw a wing shape around the middle of the bird's body.[14] You could also draw decorative shapes like stars or hearts on the bird. Just have fun!

Instead of poking holes into the clay, you could also use paint or a marker to decorate it. If you paint, use an acrylic type for the best results.

5

Flip the bird over to decorate the other side. Decorating the rest of the bird is easy. Just flip it over and draw on the other side as well. You can add an eye and wing, and any other shapes you want to.[15]

This is optional, and you don't have to decorate the other side if you don't want to.

6

Leave the clay to dry for 24 hours. Once you're all done decorating, then give your clay some time to dry. Leave it out for 24 hours and let it harden. After it's dry, you'll have a brand new clay bird decoration![16]

Dry clay is usually brittle and breaks easily, so be careful not to drop your bird.

Different clay types might need specific times to dry. Check the instructions to see how long you have to leave it out.

How to Make a Clay Horse

Crafting a clay horse is a great way to pay tribute the beloved animal and best of all you're left with your very own handmade figurine to play with or proudly display. Decide what kind of clay best suits your project and vision, wear an apron and/or clothes you don't mind getting dirty, and get ready to sculpt.

Part

1

Creating a Horse Using Modeling Clay

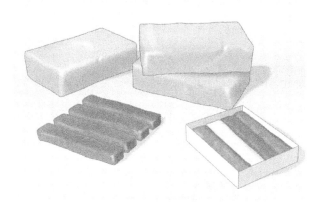

1

Determine if the type of modeling clay is the best option for your project. Many modeling clays are oil-based or wax-based, which means that they do not dry out. In fact, these clays can be exposed to air yet remain malleable for long periods of time, allowing you both to move and reshape your creations at will and to preserve your pieces for long periods of time.[1]

Modeling clay is also sturdier than a material like play-doh and typically holds its shape better, making it easier to craft more detailed pieces. [2] Note, though, that oil and wax-based modeling clays cannot be hardened, and painting these kinds of clay is not recommended.[3] If you would like to be able to paint on your clay horse, polymer clay might work better for you.

2

Prepare your work surface. Find a hard, flat surface to work on. Oil-based modeling clays can be messy and can leave greasy stains on uncovered work surfaces, so depending on how clean you'd like to keep that surface, you may find it helpful to cover your workstation with newspaper, wax paper, or saran wrap.

3

Decide how big you'd like your sculpture to be. Based on what size of horse you'd like to make your horse, estimate how much clay you'll need.

If you are new to clay modeling, you may want to avoid getting too overambitious with the scale of your horse; instead, start with a piece of clay that you can hold comfortably in one hand.

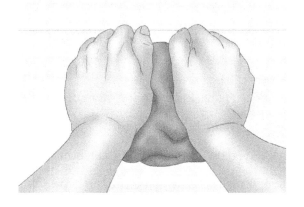

4

Knead and warm your clay. Once you've got the right amount of clay, begin either squeezing it between your hands or place the clay on your work surface and knead it like bread dough. Continue squeezing or kneading until the clay is warm, soft, and easy to work with.

5

Divide your clay into sections. Cut your clay into four pieces using a craft knife, wire clay cutter, or your hands. One piece should be slightly larger than the the other three (which should all be approximately the same size).

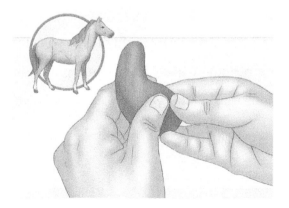

6

Model the horse's neck and torso. Take your largest piece of clay and mold it into an oblong circle. Gently pinch one end of your oblong circle and pull it upwards to form your horse's neck.

Since you'll want your horse's body to be able to support its head, be sure not make the neck too long or too thin.

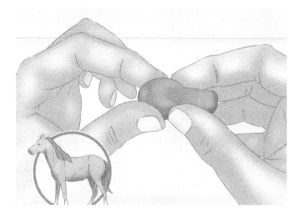

7

Form your horse's head. Begin by mold one of your three equal-sized clay pieces into a peanut shape. Next, gently pinch one end of your peanut shape, elongating it (this will be your horse's nose and mouth).

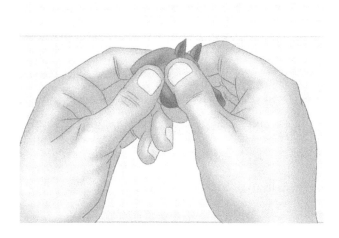

8

Create facial features. Using another one of your three equal-sized sections, craft two triangle-shaped ears and two round eyes; be sure to set aside some of this clay for your mane and tail, though. Carefully attach your eyes and ears to the larger end of the horse's head. Finally, attach your completed head to your horse's neck.

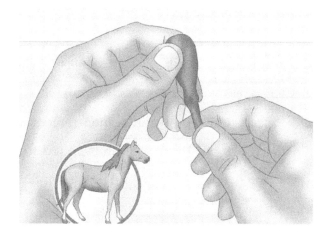

9

Mold the horse's legs. Cut your third play-doh section into four smaller pieces of equal size. Create long cylinder-shaped legs by rolling each of these pieces between your fingers until they're a length and width that look proportionate in relation to your horse's torso.

The thickness and height of your legs will depend on whether or not you'd like your horse to be able to stand upright. Thicker and shorter legs, for instance, will make for a sturdier base.

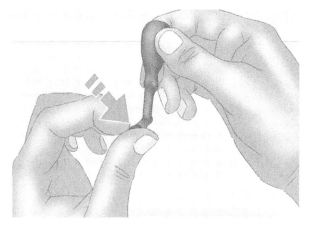

10

Mold and attach your hooves. Break off a small piece of clay from one end of each cylinder to use for your hooves. Roll each hoof into a ball. Pinch each ball between your thumb and pointer finger, making them into short cylinders. Attach one of these short cylinders to the bottom of each leg. Now attach two legs to front end of your horse's torso and two to the back end.

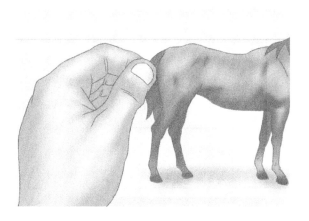

11

Add a mane and tail. Break the last of your clay into smaller pieces and form these pieces into strands or chunks of hair. To complete your horse, attach your tail to the rear end of the horse's torso and your mane to the back of the horse's head and neck and between its ears.

Part

2

Sculpting a Horse using Polymer Clay

1

Decide if polymer clay is the material that best suits your project. Pieces made from polymer clay can be put in the oven to harden (although you can also purchase air dry polymer clay), making it a good choice if preserving your sculpture is important to you.[4]

Polymer clay can also be painted, which is ideal if you are looking to create a more detailed clay model.

Keep in mind that young children should never attempt to bake their polymer creations on their own; adult supervision is always required when using an oven.

2

Get your work surface ready. Find a hard, flat surface to work on. Cover your work surface in newspaper if you are concerned with messiness.

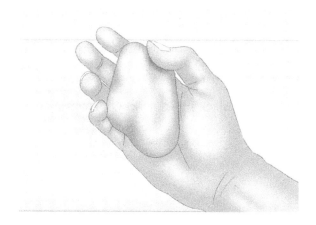

3

Figure out how much clay you'll need. While the scale of your model is ultimately up to you, remember that larger pieces will take longer to cure in the oven. We suggest that you use an amount of clay that you can hold easily in the palm of one hand.

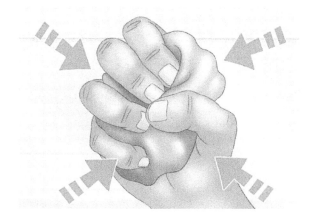

4

Warm your clay. To make your polymer clay as malleable as possible, begin by squeezing it between your hands. Work your until the clay is warm, soft, and easy to work with.

You may also choose to place the clay on your work surface and knead it like bread dough.

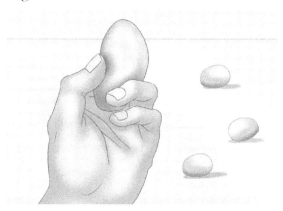

5

Separate your clay into four sections. You can use your hands, a craft knife, or a wire clay cutter to divide your clay. One of your four piece should be slightly larger than the rest, and the remaining three sections should be of roughly equal size.

6

Create your horse's neck and torso. Mold your largest piece of clay into an oblong circle. Now gently pinch one end of your oblong circle and pull it upwards to create a neck.

Make sure the neck isn't too long or too thin -- if it is it won't be able to support your horse's head.

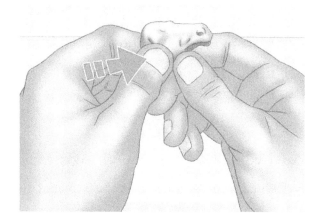

7

Mold a head. Take one of your three equal-sized clay pieces and turn it into a peanut shape. Next, gently pinch one end of your peanut shape, elongating it, to make your horse's nose and mouth.

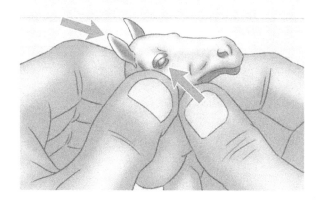

8

Create and add eyes and ears. Using another one of your three equal-sized sections, create two triangle-shaped ears and two round eyes (but be sure to set aside some of this clay for your mane and tail). Carefully fasten the eyes and ears to the larger, more round end of your horse's head. Now attach the head to your horse's neck.

9

Mold legs for your horse. Cut your third play-doh section into four smaller pieces of equal size. Roll each of these pieces between your fingers, creating long cylinders (legs), until they're a length and width that you desire.

The thickness and height of your legs should reflect whether or not you'd like your horse to be able to sturdily stand upright. Legs that are thicker and longer make for a sturdier base.

10

Mold and attach your hooves. Break off a small piece of clay from one end of each leg to create your hooves. Roll each small piece into a ball. Pinch these balls between your thumb and pointer finger until they resemble short cylinders. Attach one of these short cylinders to the bottom of each leg. Now attach two legs to front end of your horse's torso and two to the back end.

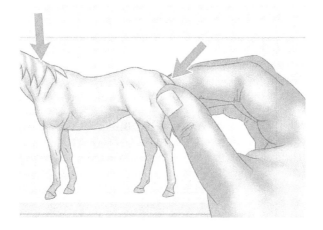

11

Use the last of your clay to make a mane and tail. Break the last of your clay into smaller pieces, forming these pieces into strands or chunks of hair. Finish modeling your horse by attach your tail to the rear end of the horse's torso and your mane to the back of the horse's head and neck and between its ears. You can omit the clay mane if you would prefer to paint one on after you've cured your sculpture.

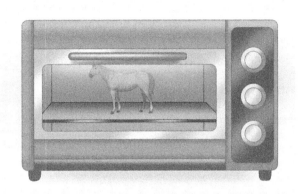

12

Cure your polymer clay horse. Follow the packet instructions to ensure that you're baking your piece at the right temperature and for the correct amount of time.

Temperatures used to cook polymer clay vary from 215°F (102°C) to 325°F (163°C). [5]

13

Choose paints that are best suited for your polymer clay. Acrylic paint is generally recommended, but if you first coat your piece with a glaze made for polymer clay (e.g. Sculpey Glaze) you may use almost any kind of paint.[6] Again, painting your horse is an entirely optional step.

14

Decide what color (or colors) you'd like to use for your horse. Many horses have spotted coats, which can be fun and a little more challenging to paint than single-colored coats. Remember, too, that while most horses found in nature are some shade of brown, beige, black, or grey, your artistic options are not as limited. If pink is your favorite color and you would like your horse's coat or mane to be pink, by all means go for it.

15

Leave your painted piece to dry. While many paints will dry in under half an hour, you may want to wait a little longer if you'd like to be on the safe side. Drying times may also vary depending on how thick a coat of paint you've applied.

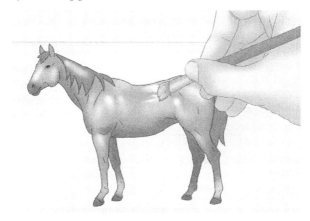

16

Apply a coat of varnish. Coating your horse with a clear varnish will help ensure that the paint maintains a fresh look and doesn't chip.[7] Be sure your paint has dried fully before you cover it with varnish, and be sure that the brush you use for your varnish coat is clean.

Part

3

Molding a Horse Using Play-doh

1

Decide if play-doh is the best material for you. Play-doh can be a great sculpting material, particularly for younger artists, but is not your best bet if you'd like to create a more long-lasting sculpture.

Play-doh is good for young sculptors because it is very soft and easy for small hands to mold.

Play-doh is also food safe, making it a wise choice for curious toddlers who might try tasting their art supplies, and is marketed as being safe for ages two and up.[8]

Unfortunately, play-doh will dry out and crack if left sitting out, so be prepared for the fact that your piece may not remain intact or in good condition for long.

2

Find a flat surface to work on. While play-doh is fairly easy to clean up, covering your work station with newspaper can make the cleaning process easier.[9]

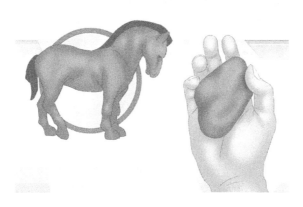

3

Determine the scale of your project. Decide how big you'd like your horse to be and estimate much play-doh you'll need accordingly.

In the interest of keeping your project manageable, you may want to avoid getting too overambitious with the size of your model. Try starting with an amount of play-doh that you can hold easily in one hand.

4

Prepare your play-doh. To ensure that your play-doh is as soft and easy to work with as possible, squeeze it between your hands until it is warm.

If you are using old play-doh that has begun to dry out, try working a small amount of water into it to restore its pliability.[10]

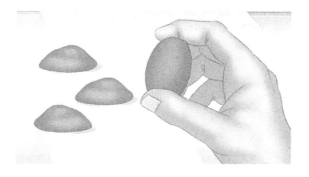

5

Divide your play-doh into sections. Using your hands, break your play-doh into four pieces, making one piece slightly larger than the rest (the other three pieces should be of roughly equal size).

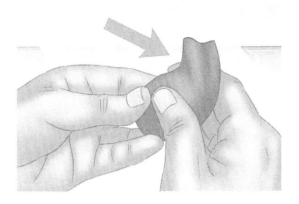

6

Model the horse's neck and torso. Take your largest piece of play-doh and mold it into an oblong circle. Gently pinch one end of your oblong circle and pull it upwards to form your horse's neck.

Since you'll want your horse's body to be able to support its head, be sure not make the neck too long or too thin.

7

Form your horse's head. Begin by mold one of your three equal-sized clay pieces into a peanut shape. Gently pinch one end of your peanut shape, elongating it, to create the horse's nose and mouth.

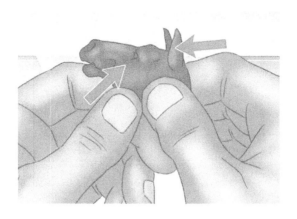

8

Create and attach facial features. Using another one of your three equal-sized sections, craft two triangle-shaped ears and two round eyes (but make sure to set aside some of this play-doh section as you will need it later to make your mane and tail). Carefully attach your eyes and ears to the larger end of the horse's head, and fasten your completed head to the horse's neck.

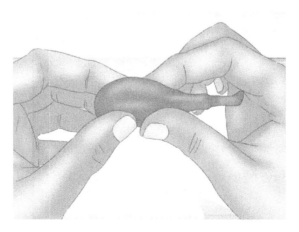

9

Make the horse's legs. Divide your third play-doh section into four smaller pieces of equal size. Roll each of these pieces between your fingers, creating long cylinder-shaped legs.

How thick you and short (or how thin and tall) you make your legs will depend on whether or not you'd like your horse to be able to stand upright. Thicker and shorter legs will make for a sturdier base.

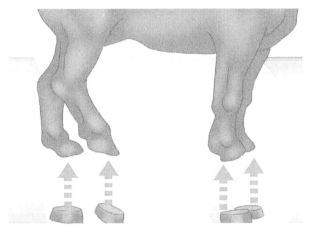

10

Mold and attach your hooves. Break off a small piece of clay from one end of each cylinder to use for your hooves. Roll each hoof into a ball, then pinch each ball between your thumb and pointer finger until they become short cylinders. Attach one of these short cylinders to the bottom of each leg, then proceed to attach two legs to front end of your horse's torso and two to the back end.

11

Add a mane and tail. Break the last of your play-doh into smaller pieces and form these pieces into strands or chunks of hair. Attach your tail to the rear end of the horse's torso and your mane to the back of the horse's head and neck and between its ears.

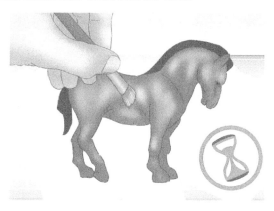

12

Allow your horse to dry and paint if desired. Play-doh is an air-drying clay, so let your piece sit out until it hardens (the drying process may take up to several days, so have patience).[11] Once your horse has dried you can add color and detail to your sculpture using either acrylic or poster paint (this is optional). [12]

Bear in mind that even if you paint it, your play-doh horse is still likely to crack or crumble after some time, as play-doh is not intended to be long-lasting.[13]

How to Create Modelling Clay Animals

The rainy season is upon us again, and there's no better time to try your hand at something creative.

Why not have a go at clay modelling? As shown by the author, Bernadette Cuxart, clay animals can be created using just three basic shapes; a ball shape, a teardrop shape and a worm shape. Cuxart's Modelling Clay Animals is an awesome little book for keeping bored, cooped-up children entertained, or for artistic types of any age who've got some spare time on their hands; you don't even need any fancy materials.

47

Why not try making a penguin? Here is how to do it:

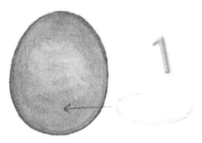

Start by rolling some black clay into an egg shape. Then, flatten out a white ball for the belly and stick it on the body.

Using orange clay (or I suppose, any colour of your choice) make two tear drop shapes for the feet. if you stick them to the bottom of the egg shape and flatten the bottoms, this will help your penguin to stand up.

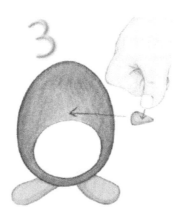

Now, make another teardrop shape which you can use for the beak.

Now for the eyes - flatten two white balls and place where you want your penguin's eyes to be. Then, flatten two smaller black balls and stick on top.

For the wings, create two sausage shapes... and flatten them! If you want, you can give her more movement by pressing just the top half of her wings on to her body. She'll look like she's moving... (almost).

And ta-da - your penguin masterpiece is complete!

Plenty more clay animal designs can be found inside this easy-to-use guide, available on our website, Amazon, Wordery and at all good book shops.

How to Make Clay Hedgehog

1.

These are the tools that you will need. You'll find a list in the "Equipment' tab above.

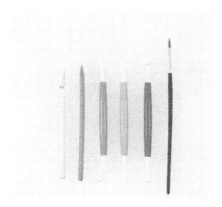

2.

Roll a 100 g ball of ivory flower paste.

3.

By pressing the ball gently in the middle and rotating, create an eight-shaped body.

4.

Gradually pinch and pull out some paste (slightly above the centre of the body) to create a nose.

5.

Press softly above the nose to make the face a little more flat.

6.

Use the frilling tool to make holes for eyes. Use the smaller side of dresden tool to mark the smile and the bigger side of tool to create the hedgehog's mouth.

7.

Roll two 3 mm balls of black flower paste and stick them in the previously made holes. Deepen the smile lines with a sharp scalpel.

8.

Make an oval shape out of a 4 mm ball of black flower paste and stick it as a nose. Roll a 2 mm ball of black flower paste and put it in the figure's mouth. Using the bigger side of dresden tool flatten the black paste.

9.

To create the hedgehog's spines form teardrop shapes from brown flower paste. Start with the first row of longer spines on top of the head (7 mm-10 mm balls formed into 20-25 mm long teardrops). Curve them a little. It's best to form them one at a time and stick them right away so that they don't dry. If you want to make more at a time, cover them for example with a plastic box.

10.

Move down along the sides to complete the first row. Make spines from smaller balls (about 5 mm balls).

11.'

Using the smaller side of bone tool mark places where you will stick the arms (middle of the body, next to first row of spines).

12.

Roll a 12 g ball of red flower paste. Use the bigger side of bone tool to make a hollow on top of it.

13.

Round the edge of created hollow with your finger.

14.

By pressing gently and rotating, make the bottom part of apple narrower.

15.

Use a cocktail stick to make a hole for the stalk.

16.

Glue a few flattened spines, insert a piece of a cocktail stick and stick the apple as shown on the photo.

17.

Continue by adding the next rows of spines. You might want to leave a small blank space at the back (without spines) until placing the figure on the cake. It will make it easier to move the figure without damaging the back spines.

18.

Roll a 3 g ivory ball and create a shape as shown on the photo.

19.

Press it with your finger.

20.

Use the smaller side of dresden tool to mark two lines on the thicker side of element. You want the lines to end where the hollowing starts. Begin with shallow lines, then deepen them a little.

21.

Mark three curved lines where the indentation starts to create toes.

22.

Use a sharp scalpel to make a cut along the two lines shown in the step 20.

23.

Use a ball tool to make shallow holes in the centre of the foot. Repeat steps 18-23 for the second foot.

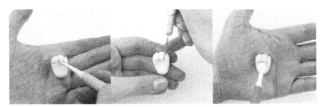

24.

Roll two 5 mm balls of dusky pink flower paste...

25.

... and press them into the holes made in the previous step.

26.

Stick the feet to the body.

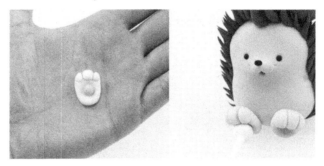

27.

For each arm you will need 1 g (1 cm ball) of ivory flower paste. Dip the wire in glue and wipe off the excess. Roll a 2 cm sausage and insert the wire to about its two third's.

28.

Hold the sausage in between your fingers and roll it softly to make a narrowing and to lengthen the arm a little.

29.

Flatten the top part.

30.

Use a scalpel to make cuts as shown on photo.

31.

Round the fingers. Cut the end of arm at an angle (the hedgehog will hold the arms up).

32.

Bring the arms close to the figure and check at what angle are they going to be inserted. Use an additional/leftover piece of wire to make an insertion at a proper angle for each arm (this way you will avoid damaging the arm while pushing it in). Stick the arms on.

33.

Make a flattened teardrop shape out of the green flower paste to create a leaf. Make a stalk out of a 2 mm ball of brown flower paste. If in the step 17 you have decided to leave the back blank, remember to keep the brown flower paste leftovers to fill the gap later.

34.

Glue the stalk and the leaf to the apple.

35.

Roll two tiny teardrop shapes out of the black flower paste to make eyebrows.

36. Finish

Made in the USA
Monee, IL
15 October 2022